To Liza!

SON OF A SEACOOK

The Story of Edith Coyer Santy

AS TOLD BY HER GRANDSON

JOSH SIMONDS

DEEP EARTH PRESS

Published by Deep Earth Press
Littleton, NH 03561

deepearthpress.com

ISBN: 979-8-9872219-0-7

© 2023 by Josh Simonds

joshsimonds.com

All Rights Reserved.

SON
OF A
SEACOOK

THE STORY OF
EDITH COYER SANTY

To my Grandmother,
Edith Helen Coyer Santy

Dedication

I didn't get to know my Gram until later on in life, well after her husband, my grandfather, passed away. The story of life got in the way of any of my grandparents being present in my childhood, and until my grandfather passed away, I didn't really know her. Once I did, my Gram became the one grandparent I *was* able to know, and come to love.

Getting to know my Gram was one of the greatest gifts life has ever given me.

Edith Helen Coyer was my Grandmother, because she was the Mother of my Mother, Kathleen Edith Santy. Edith, my Gram, would come to be known as Edith Santy, yet just like my mother herself, would always hold with pride to her maiden name of Coyer, her father's last name.

She was a Pisces like me, born in late February and I in early March. My Gram was born with a caul over her face, an indication that she had the "sight," or an old wives tale that indicated she would have spiritual insight, or what we would call psychic powers today.

Indeed, my Gram was larger than life, and she seemed to walk with the strength of 10,000 men, so her having the "sight" or some other superhuman strength wouldn't surprise me in the slightest.

I can say, from how much I got to know her, that she was truly a force of nature. She would will herself better with the strength of her mind if any ailment would ever befall her. This was true right up until the very end, when it wasn't her spirit that gave out, but her body.

My Gram always "shot from the hip," as it's said, never fearing to speak plainly. She said what was on her mind and in her heart, often without a care in the world for what others thought.

She didn't mind cussing or using swear words, or *French* as she would say. When she wanted to give someone a good ribbing, she'd refer to them as a *"son of a seacook,"* almost always preceded by a *"Put 'em up, you..."* with her fists raised up playfully. This was an old phrase and one I found so endearing, and when I was trying to think of what to call her book, that phrase jumped out at me.

My Gram was a true *"son of a seacook"* if there ever was one. Being that she wasn't afraid to fight anyone in life, man or woman, I just know she'd get a chuckle out of that.

While she was alive, she was there for me in ways that I still am incredibly grateful for, and will always be. These were the lowest points in my life, the scariest points, and she was there for me, no questions asked and no judgement given.

I hope she knows what that meant to me.

What that means to me still.

Thanks to my Gram, and getting to know her, I was able to get to know her story, her strength, and her love. As she showed me both strength and love, I know that's all she wanted for me also.

She showed that to me clearly. She showed me that, while family may be far from perfect, they're there for each other.

My life is better because she was in it, and while she was in it, she showed me what she wanted for me: strength and courage, sure, but ultimately peace and love.

That's why, as I walk through life focusing on love, health, and strength, I do so knowing that's what she would want for me, as well as all her family.

And wants for us still.

~ Edith's Grandson, Josh

ps. And to my Gram, that original *"son of a seacook"*: thank you for doing your damnedest, and showing me how to do the same. If I'm ever able to be proud of anything in my life, it will be with thanks to you.

I love you.

EDITH HELEN COYER

Born February 27th, 1931
Northfield, Vermont

Groom	Henry Joseph Coyer
Bride	Myrtle Edith Smith
Residence of Groom	Littleton, N. H.
" Bride	Littleton, N. H.
Age of Groom	24
" Bride	22
Color of Groom	White
" Bride	White
Occupation of Groom	Carpenter
" Bride	Housework
Birthplace of Groom	Woodsville, N. H.
" Bride	Montpelier, Vt.
No. of Marriage of Groom	1st
" Bride	1st
Groom Widowed or Divorced	---
Bride " " "	---
Intention Filed	July 24, 1922
By whom Married	James McKenzie
Residence	Littleton, N. H.
Official Station	Clergyman
Date of Marriage	July 29, 1922
Place	Littleton, N. H.

[Record continued over.]
*Clergyman or Justice of the Peace.

Marriage Certificate of Henry & Myrtle

DEATH OF MRS. COYER

Mrs. Myrtle E. Coyer, 36, died at her home in Northfield last Sunday morning at 12:15 o'clock after a short illness. Mrs. Coyer was born in Montpelier in 1900, the daughter of Mr. and Mrs. Edward J. Smith of Upper Main street. Mrs. Coyer resided in this city most of her life, moving to Northfield a year ago.

Mrs. Coyer is survived by her husband, Henry L. Coyer; her parents, Mr. and Mrs. Edward J. Smith of Montpelier; a five year old daughter, Edith; two brothers, Dean and Harold Smith of Burlington and by two sisters, Mrs. Henry Dion of Lisbon, N. H., and Miss Helen Smith of this city.

The funeral services were held Tuesday afternoon at 1 o'clock at the Catholic church in Northfield. The entombment was at the Green Mount cemetery in Montpelier.

Obituary of Myrtle Smith

Father: Henry Coyer
Mother: Myrtle Smith

*"Youth fades, love droops,
the leaves of friendship fall.
A mother's secret hope outlives them all."*
~ Oliver Wendell Holmes

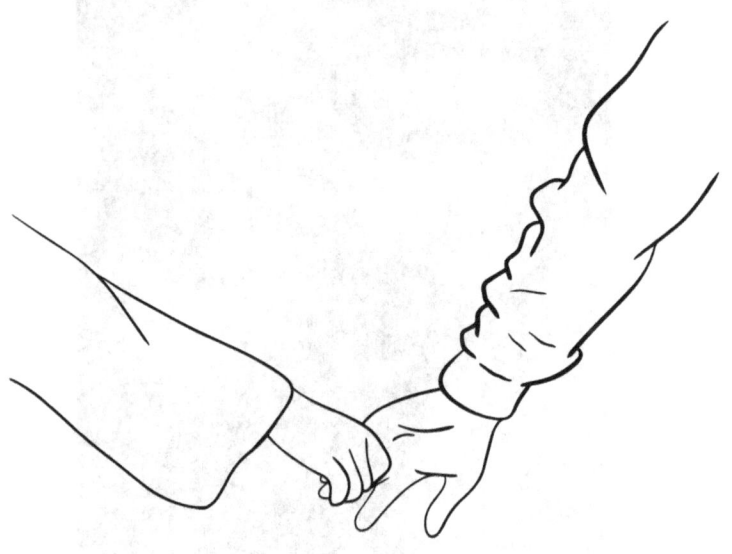

*"When my father didn't have my hand,
he had my back."*
~ Linda Poindexter

My Gram was born into a hard life right away. At the age of 5, she lost her mother Myrtle to death, and she was raised by her father, Henry, along with her grandparents for most of her childhood.

My Gram spoke of being raised in Catholic school, and was often reprimanded by the nuns for asking questions that were frowned upon.

Northfield, Vermont is near Barre, and when my Gram was growing up, her father was a stone cutter in the quarries there. She loved him very much and would recount fondly coming back from the "beer gardens" with her dad on the weekends. She had a tumultuous childhood, as she also fondly told me stories of running away from her grandparents' house at a young age to hop the train back to her dad.

She loved him fiercely, right up until he died in 1962. I know she missed her mother as well, though she hardly ever spoke of her or much of her childhood without her.

The Coyer Family

Henry's Parents, Gram's Grandparents
Eugene Coyer and Marie Zelia Dion

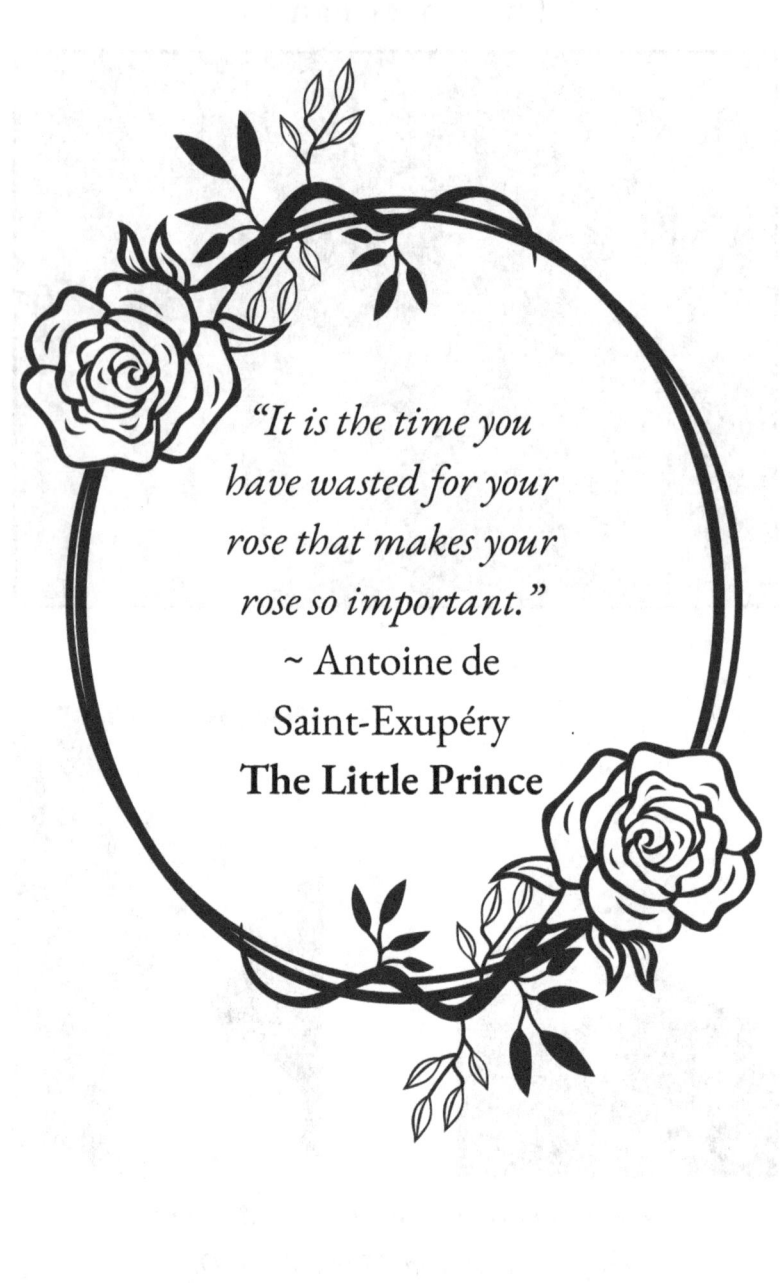

Throughout her life, she had little use for religion, or authority of any kind. This would be seen through all the ways she stood up for herself and worked for herself over her life.

My Gram's entire life was devoted to animals of all kinds. Talking to my Gram was always a wealth of stories about pets and livestock she would have.

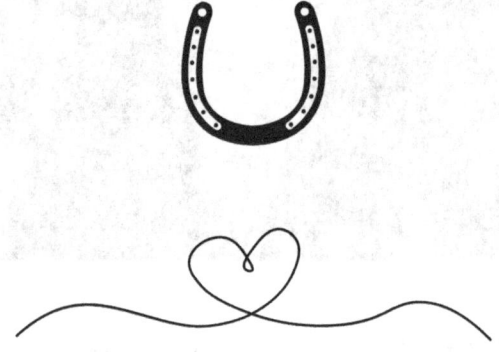

"If having a soul means being able to feel love and loyalty and gratitude, then animals are better off than a lot of humans."
~ James Herriot
All Creatures Great and Small

My Gram really saw no difference between the humans in her family, as well as her animals. In her later years, she was the old woman on the backroad that took in strays, and sadly people would take advantage of that. She had many stories of finding strange animals in her yard, or even stashed away in her vehicle with the headlights pulled on to get her attention.

She fed turkeys in her front yard, again not caring what the local wildlife officials had to say. She loved animals of all kinds her entire life.

*"You only live once,
but if you do it right,
once is enough."*
~ Mae West

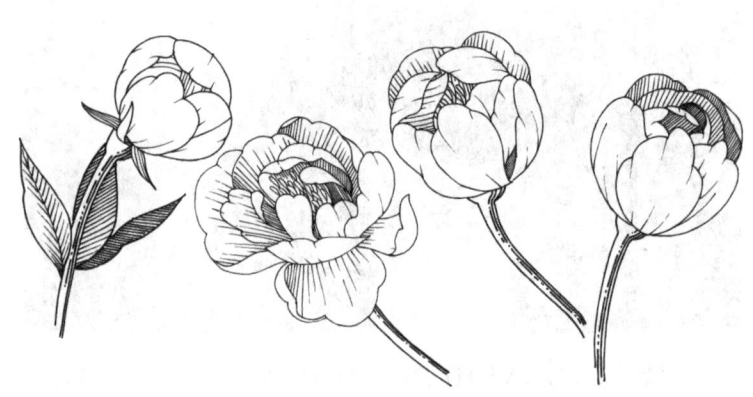

My Grandmother taught me to always question the "Shoulds" and "Supposed to's" in life. She taught me to live life on my own two feet, as an individual who stayed true to myself. I won't ever be able to thank her enough for that.

My Gram met my Grandfather, Robert Santy, while she was in her teens. They were married when she was 17, and he was 20, on December 25th, 1948.

*My Grandfather kept this picture
in his wallet his entire life.*

Bobby, Kathy, Melody, and Ricky

They had four children, the first was Robert Santy, Jr, born in 1949. Then, their second child was Melody, then Richard, then Kathleen, my mother.

They spent a life together, working together on the "Back Farm," as well as building their home on Clough Hill in Lyman. My Gram lived on Clough Hill until shortly before her death, and my Grandfather lived there until his death in October of 1998.

My Grandparents at the wedding of their son, my Uncle Ricky.

My Grandparents spent years farming and logging, scraping a living from the land.

They had years of dairy farming, and eventually my Gram moved to raising smaller animals like cats and dogs. This was her main living for many years, though she spent many years making craft items by hand, like Christmas wreaths and jewelry using porcupine quills. I don't have many memories of my grandparents from my childhood, but I always remember them coming for Christmas.

My Gram's Grandchildren

Back Row: Myself, Niki, Jay, Stevie
Front Row: Michael holding Scottie and Jessica

"Because (grandparents) are usually free to love and guide and befriend the young without having to take daily responsibility for them, they can often reach out past pride and fear of failure and close the space between generations."
~ Jimmy Carter

After my Grandfather passed in 1998, my Grandmother spent some time traveling. She met a man named Carl, who she spent a good handful of years with. This was when I really got a chance to know my Gram, as I was moving into my early 20s.

My Grandmother had a warrior spirit, respecting both Native American and "Cowboy," or anyone in whom she saw a kindred warrior spirit. She was the last one to ever back down in a fight, and this included moving on through the last half of her life and all the struggles that entailed.

Carl and Gram spent time in North Carolina, and had many adventures. She spent a lot of time visiting and learning about the Native American culture that fascinated both her and my Grandfather for so many years.

"No hour of life is wasted that is spent in the saddle."
~ *Winston Churchill*

Life isn't nearly as neat and tidy as most of the world would have us believe, and this is especially true for matters of family. I know there were reasons why I didn't have much of a childhood with my Grandparents.

Life is guaranteed to contain pain and trauma, and for some of us, that comes in greater degrees than it does for others. My mom's family life, and certainly the life of my Gram, wasn't free of it by any means.

My Gram loved spending time in the swing under her apple tree, right next to the brook that ran behind their house.

Gram with Bella

She helped instill in me that independent streak and a love of working with my hands.

A concrete casting I made for Gram

Life and circumstances, family and the sowing of oats all brought my Gram's kids on different paths. There wasn't much of my childhood that was traditional when it comes to the idea of grandparents, yet when we connected later in life, my Gram loved me with everything she had. I do understand she may have been making up for ways she would have loved less-than-perfectly as she made her way through life.

"When you look into your mother's eyes, you know that is the purest love you can find on this Earth."
~ Mitch Albom

Gram with my Uncle Bobby, August 2012

*"How you live your life is up to you.
You have to go out and grab the
world by the horns.
Rope it before it ties you down and
decides for you."*
~ Sarah Reijonen

My Gram found any opportunity to be involved in her family's lives, especially those of her great-grandchildren.

Here's my Gram, with my sister Jessica's kids, Bella & Connor.

"I could do worse than become my own grandma, or anyone of the strong women who raised us. Our strengths emerged from theirs; we build on their heritage and transform their resilience and competence into our own."

~ Regina Barreca

"You go through life wondering what is it all about but at the end of the day it's all about family."
~ Rod Stewart

*My sister Jessica's high school graduation
Left to right: my mom Kathy, Uncle Bobby, Jessica, Penny (Bobby's Girlfriend-at-the-time), my cousin Stevie, my Aunt Mel, Gram, myself, Uncle Ricky, my father Harold, my cousin Scottie*

Five Generations Strong

Gram seated with her daughter Melody, her granddaughter Niki, her great-granddaughter Nichol, and her great-great-grandchildren Kira, Karter, and Adalee

Gram with her daughter Kathy, granddaughter Jessica, and great-granddaughter Bella

Gram with her daughter Melody, granddaughter Niki, and great-granddaughter Nichol

*"The strength of a family,
like the strength of an army,
is in its loyalty to each other."*
~ Mario Puzo

"Above all, be the heroine of your life, not the victim."
~Nora Ephron

*Above:
Gram, Mom, and
Jessica June 2014*

*Left:
Gram and Bella at
Bella's Dance
Recital June 2013*

"Love is patient, love is kind. It does not envy, it does not boast, it is not proud. It does not dishonor others, it is not self-seeking, it is not easily angered, it keeps no record of wrongs. Love does not delight in evil but rejoices with the truth. It always protects, always trusts, always hopes, always perseveres. Love never fails."

~ 1 Corinthians 13:4-8

"Age does not protect you from love, but love to some extent protects you from age."
~Jeanne Moreau

Above:
Gram, Jess, and kids at Gram's 80th birthday party, February 2011

Right:
Aunt Mel & Gram at Bella's Birthday Party

Gram and Family June 2014

Left to Right:
Mike, Jessica, Connor, myself,
Gram in front, Kathy, Harold, Bella

"Family is not an important thing. It's everything."
~Michael J. Fox

Top to Bottom: Gram with Bella, Connor, and Sequoia

Gram continued on into her Eighties, having fun and visiting with her family as often as she could. She continued to enjoy her home and her time with her animals, as well as any project she decided to take on at the time.

Gram with her sister, Carol, at Gram's 80th Birthday Party

*Left:
Gram and
Bella*

*Below:
Gram,
Mom, and
Connor*

"Grandmother. The true power behind the power." ~ Lisa Birnbach

Gram and Bella

"It is not the honor that you take with you, but the heritage you leave behind."
~ Branch Rickey

Aunt Mel and Gram

"I won't be wronged. I won't be insulted. I won't be laid a-hand on. I don't do these things to other people, and I require the same from them."

~ John Wayne

Gram and my Dad, Harold

Gram and Mike

My Gram and I in September, 2011

My Gram had the fiercest heart I ever knew. While she didn't talk much about her life growing up, I know she suffered through incredible hardships. Over the course of her life, she experienced the worst any human could: she buried her parents, her husband, and two sons.

She was a fighter like none I've ever known.

"The love for all living creatures is the most noble attribute of man."
~ Charles Darwin

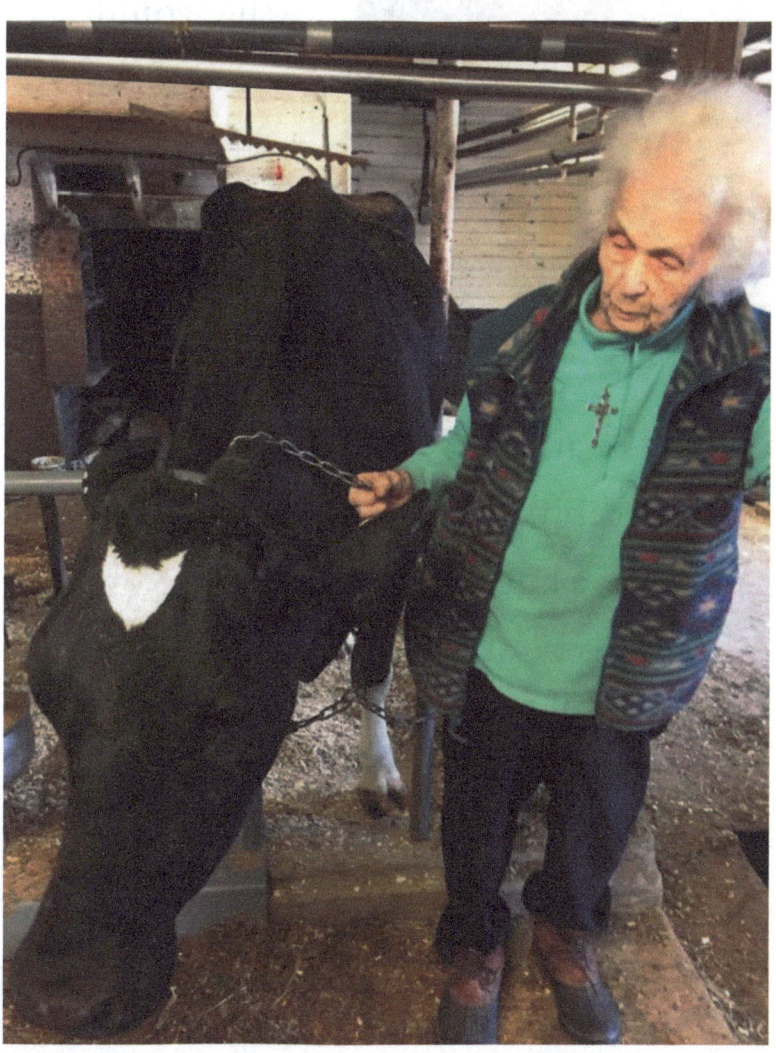

If my Gram could,
she would.
And if she couldn't, she'd still find a way.

We are so incredibly lucky to have known her, to be able to call her Mother, Grandmother, and Great-grandmother.

Her spirit was fierce and her mind sharp, even as she grew older and her body began to fade.

"To live in hearts we leave behind is not to die."

~ Thomas Campbell

Eventually my Gram reached the point all of us do - where our bodies are no longer strong enough to keep us in this world.

My parents and my Aunt Mel selflessly opened up their homes to my Gram in her final days, giving her an opportunity to make her transition surrounded by those she loved. I'll forever be grateful to them for that, as well as everyone who helped her make her transition with dignity, strength, and peace.

*Top to Bottom:
Gram and Nichol,
Gram with Bella
and Connor,
and Gram with
Niki*

"You will lose someone you can't live without, and your heart will be badly broken, and the bad news is that you never completely get over the loss of your beloved. But this is also the good news. They live forever in your broken heart that doesn't seal back up. And you come through. It's like having a broken leg that never heals perfectly - that still hurts when the weather gets cold, but you learn to dance with the limp."

~ Anne Lamott

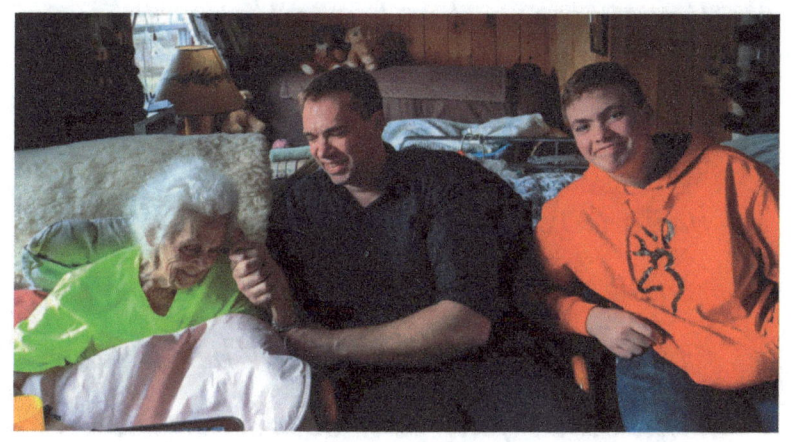

In her last days, Sequoia, myself, and the rest of our family spent as much time with her as we could.

Her wisdom, strength, and love live on in us still.

"I'm gone now, but I'm still very near, death can never separate us. Each time you feel a gentle breeze, it's my hand caressing your face. Each time the wind blows, it carries my voice whispering your name. When the wind blows your hair ever so slightly, think of it as me pushing a few stray hairs back in place. When you feel a few raindrops fall on your face, it's me placing soft kisses. At night look up in the sky and see the stars shining so brightly. I'm one of those stars and I'm winking at you and smiling with delight. For never forget, you're the apple of my eye."

~ Mary M. Green

My Gram showed me how fiercely someone can love and protect those they love. She was fiercely intelligent, incredibly loving, and a force of nature to be reckoned with.

Tenacity, strength, humor, talent, intelligence, wit, and love.

I'll never forget her.

My Gram passed away on June 19th, 2018, in a way only she would: by herself. She waited until everyone was out of the room and then quietly slipped away, to the place where her parents, her sons, and all her loved ones were waiting for her.

From that place, I know she watches over us, wanting for us what she wanted in life.

Love. Joy. Peace.

And if that's all I can do to help her rest in peace, is for me to truly live in peace?

I'm happy to oblige.

We followed through with my Gram's wishes, spreading her ashes in the brook behind her house, taking the opportunity to finally spread Bobby's ashes as well. We gathered for a day of food, laughter, and remembrance (and of course the tears she wouldn't want us to shed.) Walking behind her house, headed to the brook, I asked her if she was there with us.

I look down and find this four-leaf clover. Of course she was.

Of course she was.

Before my Gram passed away, her friend Debbie encouraged her to write some of her poetry down. After my Gram passed, Debbie sent what she had to my sister.

What follows here is that poetry, both transcribed and in her handwriting.

Thanks to my sister, Jessica, for providing not only that poetry but with pictures, dates, and help with this book. I can only imagine how happy Gram is with us for kicking ass in the ways only her grandchildren could. Love ya, sis. Keep kicking ass.

She'd only want it that way.

To My Daughters

When you're sick, I wish you well.

When you're sad, I wish you happiness.

When you're broke, I wish you gold.

When you're old, I wish you youth.

When you go on a trip, I wish you safe return,

Always and forever my love,

for you will remain the same.

To My Sons

Why am I here, I live and breathe but I'm not alive, half of me has died. I don't look for tomorrow, it could be filled with sorrow. I know I'm not alone walking down this road. There's no signs of the pain I've seen, but believe me it's there, there's no bondage or broken bones, just a broken heart. No doctor can repair it, it's mine to ear until death I depart, but love is stronger and until we meet again in a better place and I'll again see the smile on your face, saying "Hi Mom, we've saved you a place."

To My Sons

Why am I here, I live and breath but I'm not alive, half of me has died. I don't look for tomorrow it could be filled with sorrow. I know I'm not alone walking down this road, there no signs of the pain I bear, but believe me it's there, there no bandages or broken bones, just a broken heart. No doctor can repair it, its mine to bear until death I depart, but love is stronger and until we meet again in a better place and I'll again see the smile on your face, saying Hi mom we've saved you a place.

I Wish

I wish I was young again
I wish I was pretty
I wish I was rich and witty
I wish not to be lonely
I wish not to be sad
I wish for true love only
If wishes could come true
I'd be forever with you

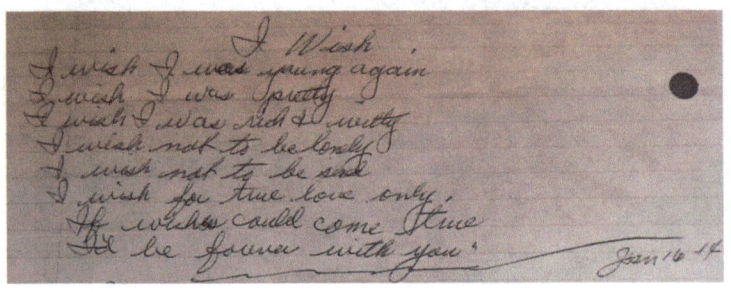

Until We're All Together Again

This life goes on, until the end.
Only this much I know as God is my witness, and to my friends know for now I'll say,
"See you later."
We'll be together again.
God has separated us in life but we'll be together in eternity when this life ends.

See you later,

Mom

Heaven Can Wait

Life is full of surprises, some good some bad,
some make us happy, some make us sad.
I've enjoyed it all, my family and friends,
the good times not the bad.
Now the time left grows short, my family chain is broken.
Somehow, somewhere, it'll be put together again,
until we're all together and the chain repaired,
live and love today, that's all we have,
there's no definite date so
Heaven can wait.

Heaven Can Wait

Life is full of surprises, some good some bad. Some make us happy some make us sad. I've enjoyed it all, my family and friends, the good times not the bad.

Now the time left grows short, my family chain is broken. Somehow, someway it'll be put together again. Until we're all together and the chain repaired live & love today, that's all we have, there's no definite date so

Heaven can wait